SURFACE  *I*

Surface Tension

ELISABETH ROWE

PETERLOO POETS

First published in 2003
by Peterloo Poets
The Old Chapel, Sand Lane, Calstock, Cornwall PL18 9QX, U.K.

**A catalogue record for this book is available
from the British Library**

ISBN   1-904324-10-X

Printed in Great Britain By
Antony Rowe Ltd, Chippenham, Wilts.

ACKNOWLEDGEMENTS

'Founder Members of the Mothers' Union' is taken from a photograph of that title dated 1876 at Old Alresford House, Hants.

'Sauna by the Lake' and Pyhaniemi: noon' appeared in the *Poetry on the Lake* anthology 2001.

'Swimming the Horse to Mull' won 4th Prize in the Peterloo Poets Open Poetry Competition 2003.

For A.G.W. who wore black

Contents

Size Isn't Everything

Size isn't everything
unless of course you happen to be small.
Size and supremacy make bullies of us all.

In the beginning is the playground pinch
plumping the forearm where it hurts the most;
the poison tips of sibling arrows,
mute endurance of blue shins under grey flannel.

The bully-boys of history learn early
that big boots disguise small imaginations;
and many will bend eagerly to lick
and many will bruise easily and die.

Mother countries eat their cubs,
grow fat and territorial, swipe minorities
with honeyed paw.

Now at the shrinking end of life
waiting the boot-crunch of eternity,
it's time to be sorry

for smaller things betrayed:
for worms beheaded curiously in play
for centipedes brushed back into hot ashes

for flies bludgeoned with rolled newspaper,
workoholic ants casually made redundant,
wasps drowning in cider;

time to atone for
children with haunted faces,
innocent spiders elegantly murdered in
a coriolis spiral down the plughole.

The Diaries

One for each year of her life
in a cardboard box in chronological order
from nineteen thirty something.

Nothing to indicate the wider picture,
convulsions of history in the making,
the war and that sort of thing.

Each day an ordinary happening
a trip to the seaside, somebody's half term
a hundred hot cross buns.

Hard to see why she bothered, really:
you could search volumes in vain for useful insights
into her essential self.

You wouldn't discover that she was allergic
to shellfish and cats and abstained absolutely
from chocolate and pessimism

but was addicted to bluebells and the salt sea smell
and a certain make of bloomers from Torquay
the colour of mushroom gills.

You wouldn't learn that she could sniff out
last night's fag at fifteen paces, was teetotal
barring a few gins and tonic

and insisted on reading aloud her notes from
geology evening classes and blatantly favoured
one particular grandchild.

You could find no mention of her morphine madness
or the fact that she waited till people had opened
their Christmas presents before dying

or why she left behind a dozen identical brown
quilted anoraks and every single letter she had
ever received from anyone.

You wouldn't guess either what the little stars stood for
alongside some of the dates e.g. August 1940
nine months before I was born.

My Father

I am older than my father when he died,
yet what I remember chiefly
are the childish things:

how he jiggled the palm of his hand
against his ear
and made a mouse squeak there;

how he cupped hands and blew
between his thumbs
to summon cuckoos in the bluebell woods;

how he drove me to buy cider
for a Sunday treat,
and I poked my head up through the sunroof
singing to the wind,
face peppered with insects;

how he made me shut my eyes at bedtime,
flew me to Cairo on a magic carpet,
where disaffected camels grunted,
nuzzling my neck,
and wild-eyed merchants wheedled me
with sweetmeats in the souk;

how he was sad when he walloped me, just once,
and when he slunk out to the garage
to smoke his pipe.

One day after mowing the wet lawn
he took his indigestion pills and died.
They all said nothing could have saved him:
I could, said my mother, had I known
anything about cholesterol.

I was a grown woman when my father died
but recollection renders me a child,
even when I try to conjure him with sherry
drunk from his grown-up crystal;
or sniff his mustard yellow waistcoat
for adult clues.
Always when I fling my arms around his memory
he holds a young girl tight against
his unconditional rock solid love.

Confession

Once I stole a small cut glass salt cellar
from a boring shop in Sheringham:
I took a fancy to it,
cycled home past the wide accusing marshes
bent like a bed of reeds.
All night the huge policemen stalked my dreams.
Next day I cycled back,
found the small disc of guilt in a film of dust
and put the damn thing back.

Once a hot water bottle burst in my grandmother's bed:
I folded the rubbery stained sheets
beneath my child's body
and slept in shame.

Once I went to church to stare prayerless
at the priest's fingers, lusting religiously.

Once I superimposed another's face on the face of love,
bit blood to stop another's name escaping.

Once I faked it – well actually, more than once.

Once, perched on a branch that overhung
the old A 20, I dropped an apple
straight through the sunroof of a passing car,
watched juices splitting, the car swerving madly,
tasted a murderous joy.

Once I touched my father's dead face
in the coffin in the morning room;
his flesh dimpled like pressed dough
and would not rise again.

The Dare

The afternoon plum-heavy, waspish;
the lane spattered with cowslick,
loose khaki splats of cudded
and sweetly curdled Kentish grass.

My tenth year of middling between
two brothers, who come skirmishing
through the limp grasses, cornstalks
dangling from their mafia mouths.

The nettles, shoulder high and listless,
crisp their hairy tips for the stinging,
the ten seconds of sibling trial,
my bare-legged dare, my orchard glory.

Pigeons croon from the barn roof.
My skin erupts in a white hot rash:
I stoop to hide my triumph, scratch
under the straps of my summer sandals.

Leaves on the Line

Late in the season.
Rain, and leaves on the line:
the train dawdling.

Ducks swimming the fields;
a tight weave of winter wheat
luminous green.

I travel back to the engine
in the manner approved by my mother
in case of accident

watching the world in retreat,
bright fragments streaking to vanishing point,
the here and now emptying.

Better to sit face forward,
my father said: welcome the loom of landscape
air punch of tunnel,

the here and now filling,
the future visibly curving along lines
that gleam like solder.

I press my temple to the cool glass.
A yellow leaf clings to the window
and spins away.

A thousand sharp facets of turned earth
catch the falling sun
and toss back gold.

Mother and Daughter

The mother flutters round the carriage
like a bird trapped in a room,
disposing daughter, suitcase, dog,
and polystyrene cups
of bitter coffee.

She talks in short sharp shocks.
'What is a Bunsen burner?
You won't pass your chemistry exam
if you don't revise.'

She leaps up, moves things
from here to there and back again.
A restless game, its rules
unfathomable.

The daughter listens as one listens
to a distant door that is banging, banging...
In the tense set of her shoulders
she is already her mother,
but being a daughter, she rolls her eyes,
presses her bloodless knuckles to the cup
and squirms appropriately;

and as the train slows
to another unscheduled stop
where someone has written
'Railtrack is shite' on the bridge,
she stares at the leggy mustard flowers
making yellow festival
and pretends she is somewhere else.

Founder Members of the Mother's Union 1876

Oh you Victorian ladies of comfortable years
you gaze from your perpetual sepia captivity
with discomforting plainness.

Seated in the front row in corseted formation
the seven most formidable of your fellowship
fidget with loosely folded hands.

Each one of you dwarfed by a heavy burden
of sober garmentry in which your female
shapeliness is quite effaced.

Sensible dark skirts sweep to the floor, voluminous
fringed capes conceal your ample bosoms;
bonnets enhance matronliness.

It is hard to read the expressions on the waxen moons
of your over-exposed faces but your lips are tight
and your smiles are still-born.

Impossible to guess what if anything you might know
of veniality, of playfulness or loving-kindness
and the soft motherly virtues.

Impossible to conceive of the act of union that
made you mothers yet there are certain well disguised
signs of amused dissension:

a toe peeping out from a wide striped skirt,
a jaunty hat with an ostrich plume that sabotages
your dutiful high seriousness.

Oh you eighteen godly matrons your moribund seemliness
does not altogether convince: go home, loosen your hair
learn to be women again.

You Wore Black

You wore black for gravitas and not, alas,
for mourning all the sweet forbidden things.
I hated the gloomy cloth that flapped around
your Presbyterian limbs, revealing wrists
embarrassingly thin, and your black shoes
shiny with probity. I longed to release you
from your virginal collared bondage: all that
imperturbable uprightness made me
queasy with desire.

I forgave the way your thick black hair
was going absent without leave, would have
drowned myself in the peat pools of your eyes,
would have sold my soul for those deep ox eyes
and your bright oxblood lips, your beautiful hands
and your dark chocolate voice leading me
into temptation.

So it was not very nice to find myself jilted
for the Bride of Christ. You offered me agape
not eros, and I should have been grateful.
You couldn't have known that the knife had cut
at the tender growing point and that my hand
would return again and again to the scar.

Out of Your Mind

Think of a painter, a pointillist,
assembling your features with a hundred thousand
painstaking touches of colour,
dotting you into existence.
Now think of the process in reverse:
watch your tight integrated ego
spin off into fragments,
uncomposing you.
They call it having a breakdown.

Think of a tent
and the rain all night on the nylon roof
and the ooze under your groundsheet;
thick mist outside, orange after the green tent,
and the absolute pointlessness of getting out
of your sleeping bag, even though that too is wet.
They call it feeling under the weather.

Think of a trough of low pressure
approaching in nauseous wavy lines
fronted with spikes:
depression, that old Icelandic dog,
your faithful companion.
Bad weather ahead, wild days and windblown nights;
poor visibility and heavy tearfall.

Imagine yourself as a ripe fruit,
a paw-paw perhaps or a pomegranate
hanging by a fragile stalk:
think how you will split in the cruel sun
how all your bright seeds will burst into oblivion
not even one to root itself for your re-birth.
They call it falling apart.

Think of losing someone you love
and the sudden unimportance
of all those things you were just about to do
and the lassitude that comes to
anaesthetise the pain; and how all the little losses
you'd carefully forgotten
come jostling your darkened memory
for their own space.
They call it being half out of your mind.

Relativity

The giant stop-watch at the swimming pool
blearily jerks a circular dot-to-dot design
for every used-up second of my life,
counting me down to oblivion.

In the black quilted limbo of night
the luminous second hand of my watch
goes on its spooky millimetred round
of all my unregarded hours.

Time's conspiracy, to render visible
the re-cycling of my own mortality,
beguiling as a comfort blanket
ragged with constant washing.

If I were to measure end to end
each hopscotch leap of time,
my life might stretch to Timbuctu,
Papua New Guinea, or Murmansk.

I listen to a man giving a lecture
unravelling relativity:
something about bending time
to accommodate space.

I'm skeetering over the surface of things
like a water boatman spread-eagled
on the mirrored sky, sustained only by the
slimmest margin of surface tension.

What Is Lost

What is lost
is the casual alchemy
of sounds becoming words:
the taken for granted metamorphosis
of a shared language,
ordinary speech tossed to and fro
between friends or those who might have become friends.

I watch words take shape on your lips
and hear them float across the space
between our faces,
rhythm and cadence still intact
but sense uncoupled somewhere.
Meaning has gone absent without leave.

The kingdom of my mind
has closed its borders:
only a few words of the pushier kind
will force the hearing frontier
leaving a jostling crowd behind, disconsolate,
their message inaccessible
their sound muffled.

I have strategy of nods and smiles
and like a well-trained actor I rehearse
my repertoire of interested murmurs,
but the musician must have his accompanist
and point its counterpoint.

What is lost is both simple and profound:
the making of connections,
something I never gave much thought to before.

Absence more painful than the other losses:
the distant shout of the first cuckoo
the music of the valley after rain
a grandchild discovering another word.

One in a Thousand

We flail among the dark entanglements of
thoughts unthinkable,
forbidden impulses,
wanting only what is not.

Someone has to be the one in a thousand
but statistics being treacherous and glib
we are not prepared.

Her funny screwed-up eyes
her folded ears, her tiny
disapproving down-turned mouth
signal her difference.

Back into the cupboard go the moses basket
and the home-made mobile.

Then there is nothing but the waiting
and the knowing that her half-imagined life
will come to us muffled
like wind chimes in someone
else's garden.

Addiction

They should have labelled him with
a government warning:
'Loving can seriously damage your health.'

She wouldn't have listened,
so cool, so beguiling the breathing in,
the sweet nicotine kick,
all the fun of the oral fixation:
it was grown-up and it gave her
something to do with her hands.

She was just getting the hang of it,
no longer gagging or wheezing,
so hip, so theatrical the breathing out,
casting smoke rings like a café sophisticate,
when he buggered off.

She sent signals from time to time;
he kept turning up like a trapper
deft with the snare.
She lent her dependency to gumsters, patchers, hypnotists.
How many therapists does it take to change a light bulb?
One but the bulb must really want to change.

Oh narcotic love!
So dark, so satisfying the surrender,
the deep deep drag! She ignored mortality
lurking like an old quack in the corner,
perking up at the sight of one more
suicide lover sooting her lungs.

If he had been just another bad habit
she would have given him up:
it was the craving she couldn't hack,
the craving.

Nice Girls

Where have all the nice girls gone?
The ones who smiled with perfect post-war teeth
and laughed their bright metallic laughs
admiringly;
who meted out their fleshly favours inch by inch
in the back row of cinemas
and knew how far to go.

Whatever happened to the nice girls?
The ones who shyly held your hand and needed
coaching in French kissing;
who practised virginity with legs and fingers crossed,
elasticated armour
and morals stiff as hairspray
on their back-combed pageboy helmets.

Where are they now, all those nice girls?
The ones who didn't bare their navel studs
and waxed bikini lines;
who didn't aim their nipples in your face
or keep condoms on their key-rings;
who knew that everything depended on
not being That Sort Of Girl.

It was more fun with the nice girls:
you had to learn rules of combat in the war
of coyness attrition,
where victory was a furtive hand down the blouse
or a finger in the zone marked
Heavy Petting.

They're probably extinct, all the nice girls,
all but a few making up for lost time
in their second adolescence:
painting their toenails, ogling toyboys,
licking ice cream cornets in the street,
wearing wet T-shirts and practising
guiltless promiscuity.

Their louche testosterone-toasted boys
are slack and balding now,
leering at girls with grinning midriffs, tattoos
and not so nice behaviour;
nursing a secret longing for the days
before each body carried its own health warning;
when innocence was aphrodisiac
and each 'No Trespassing' sign
an invitation more irresistible than
acres of naked flesh.

Picnic at Uffington

He looks like a man of flint
kneeling on the tartan rug
crushing harebells
but she is optimistic.

Underneath her twinset
breathes bawderie anglaise
straps pizzicato taut
skin white as junket.

The tongue sandwiches are
seasoned with chalk.
She licks her lips to
moisten the shyness.

He's forgotten the corkscrew
but he improvises
with a penknife
bloodying the cork.

This is not the hanky-panky
she has in mind and
furthermore she sees
that any picknickering

will be tricky with
a sore thumb and that only
harebells are destined for
deflowering today

so she follows him meekly
down the grass mountain
into the blinding belly
of the horse.

Aconites

Plant them in the green, you said, and handed me
a small unpromising bundle of loam
and limp yellowing leaves.

I shape a hollow, shifting the perfect skeletons
of last year's leaf-fall,
firming unmatched earth round the floppy stems.

The aconites, unmoved by summer's ferment,
autumn feast and winter fastness,
draw to the centre.

Not till the blackthorn breaks along the hedge
and the sun sits cold upon the hill
in the lean brown March time of another year
will they awaken,
sharpen their golden blades to slice their way
upwards to spring.

No less a miracle, I said, that love,
buried in the green,
having gathered to itself the bitter juices of neglect
and learned the dark intimacy of roots

hardens to a long sleep: biding the time
when hidden shoots, hungry for light and air,
begin to split and wander,

jostling just on the turn to green
upwards to light.

The Marrow

I am peeling a marrow,
flaying it with a minimalist
potato peeler
shaped like a lyre.

It strips like green and white striped
vinyl wall paper,
rasps like the sharkskin tablecloths
our grandmothers used
to soften the marble.

I think of the long soft whiteness of your arms

make a chisel of my fingertips,
gouge out the spongy mush
hopeful with little seeds

slice glistening half-moons
into the pan
remembering
how little water a marrow needs
after its long thirst.

This Thing

This thing arrived unbidden
like a spiky epiphyte on a high wire
feeding on air.

I gave it hospitality
and now
it has taken possession.

Do not be old: wait,
let me catch up with you.

I've only just learned
to fit my cheek
to your hollow chest

eavesdrop on your
heart's doggedness

have yet to memorise
skin's history
bone's geography.

I watch you bend
to tie your laces:

your scalp smells like an infant's.

At each parting I hear
only gongs and tumbrels.

The tree waits to be shaken
but no winds come.

After you are dead

After you are dead
do not expect to find me
veiled and weeping behind a pillar
or skulking among gravestones
like a mistress.

I shall be laying you out
in some strong room of the heart
resting my cheek on the prow of your ribcage
still warm to my touch.

I shall be setting out the little gifts in a row
to make my shrine.

And then I shall be running wild among
the high places and the screaming cliffs

lighting huge beacons
so that your soul shall pass my way
on its outward journey.

You biquitous

being not there
you are everywhere

sculpted from fragments
culled among strangers

rogue sheaf of hair
that will not lie flat

shadowed recess at the
edge of curved mouth

white cuff liberated
from a black sleeve

imagined indentations
on an empty bed

ghostly dusting of skin's
deciduousness

thin persistent tinnitus
ribcage nagging

you being not here

Silly Boy

I didn't ask him to come down here
looking for me:
I was quite happy, actually,
wandering the banks of Styx
taking the odd boat trip,
walking that big sloppy dog,
kipping in fields of asphodel.

I wish he hadn't come down here
pining for me,
twanging his wretched lyre the whole night long
getting on everyone's nerves.
I'd got used to the underground,
never having to turn on the central heating
or wonder what the weather will be like.

I didn't need him to come down here
asking for me.
It's quite cosy if you don't mind the dark,
and always warm enough to wear a T-shirt.
Being the king's favourite and young,
I have to put up with getting stared at,
and a few women are downright resentful.

I wish he hadn't come down here
unsettling me,
smelling of sweet unsulphured breezes,
brushing the luminous green stalks
of new corn from his hair.
He'd even remembered to bring my total sunblock!
Silly boy, he shouldn't have looked back.

Surprise Me

Surprise me:
burn up to my front door one day
on a black and silver Harley Davidson
and pulling off your gauntlets declaim:
'I'm taking you out for a slap-up fuck this evening;
starters, afters, the works!'
Gather me up under one tattooed arm
straddle me pillion
and rev off into the night
eating up cats' eyes at one
hundred miles an hour.
Or, if that seems beyond the call of duty,
pick up the phone, why not?

Surprise me:
gallop up to my garden gate one day
on a seventeen hands white stallion
and regarding me from a great height, declare:
'You shall be my assistant escort of the bedchamber
starting immediately!'
Pluck me up with one slash-sleeved arm,
settle me side-saddle
and whinny off into the night,
sparks flying from all four hooves
wind honing our faces:
or, if that seems a bit extravagant,
drop me a line, why not?

Soul Mates

Slim intelligent linguistic pedant
W L T M (would like to meet)
person of similar endangered species
to share fun times and poss 1 t r'ship;
someone incapable
of ending a sentence with a preposition
mangling the past tense of the verb 'to lay'
or saying different than:
someone up with whom I should not easily become fed.

Old fashioned profess grad grammarian
W L T M (would like to meet)
someone with similar passionate interest
in serious sentence analysis and parsing.
Someone compatible
to eschew estuary accent and exchange
tender linguistic care:
someone for whom correctness is something on by which
he or she can easily become turned.

Stylish affectionate linguistic purist
W L T M (would like to meet)
person to share good times in ivory tower
and experiment with subordinate clauses.
Someone prepared to
tolerate all my subjunctive moods,
abjure all bastard American spellings
and on a desert island choose the Bible,
Shakespeare and Fowler's *Use of English*.

Pun-loving athletic linguistic rhetorician
W L T M (would like to meet)
person for whom romance denotes
an etymological origin.
Someone devoted to
the music of colon and semi-colon;
who, when the captain of the sinking ship
cries, 'Every man for themselves!'
feels the need to make kindly corrections.

Lonely disillusioned linguistic dodo
W H L T M (would have liked to meet)
bubbly attractive articulate stickler
for whom imperfect is merely a tense
but will settle for
anyone with N S O H (no sense of humour)
who will end a sentence with a proposition
to regularly make passionate love with
with a view to f 'ship or just getting lain.

Stone Angels

I know the ones you mean:
one on either side of the transept
just where the roof vaults crouch
for their gravity-defying leap of faith.

Hard to imagine the ropes and pulleys
that hauled the stone up there
and the stone masons dropping one by one
from the scaffolding like fallen angels.

It hurts my neck now to watch
their trumpeting, unseen below by the shuffling
queues processing (clockwise, please)
past the cosy shrines, inhaling sanctity.

I don't believe you should have to pay
to enter the house of God, do you?
but someone has to be responsible for
the upkeep of the place and cleaning the angels.

And the last bloke to do it said, apparently,
that their blank chiseled eyes were fixed
on each other and there were signs that it wasn't
purely the love of God they were celebrating.

I wouldn't know: I can hardly see them now.
I can hardly even manage the down-to-earth
sort of jubilation, and my own wings
are corroding with incense and traffic fumes.

Close Encounter

The voice informs us smoothly
that we are now flying at thirty thousand feet.
All three hundred passengers fear that
we are in the wrong place altogether.

Lethargic on re-cycled air and cheap wine
and bored with dollies' picnics
we are not re-assured to find our captain thinks
he's something of a joker.

'Do you believe in flight?' he asks
as we encounter sudden turbulence
the plane a bucking bronco.
'Yes!' we affirm in unison like never-never children.

Forget aero-dynamics, surely we know that
only the sheer will of three hundred people
keeps the plane skyborne till at last
the voice informs us smoothly

that we shall shortly be beginning our descent
and that the weather at our destination
is clement for the time of year
and death waits in the transit lounge for a later flight.

The Philosopher

The Philosopher leans across to cadge tabacco.
his perfectly smooth bald head gleams
under the sodium lighting. We shuffle chairs.

After two brandies, modestly he confides
his grand design: a synthesis of all
philosophies. 'Personally,' he says,

'I incline to the Aristotelian persuasion.'
'Remind me,' I ask politely, 'roughly speaking,
what defines Aristotle's point of view?'

At the next table a woman eats alone,
feeding a white poodle. I condemn her
for her leopard-skin jeans, her gold sandals,

her Bardot pout. I am talking philosophy
but I can tell the man is not impressed.
He prods his pipe, weighs my seriousness.

'He loved order in the natural world
in which all things had their own form and purpose.
He saw beauty in the middle way,

nothing to excess, all things in perfect balance.'
I watch, mesmerised, his thin beautiful hands
make arabesques in the smoky air,

sculpting abstractions. I can't help noticing
how all the ologies and isms sound sexier
in French. Pinioned by his earnestness

I nod, wisely. 'I want to make philosophy
accessible,' he says, 'to the common man.'
His eyes slide sideways to the common woman.

'I submit each chapter to public scrutiny
and study each response.' I fear his task
is Sisyphean, perhaps he's a little crazy.

Suddenly the woman catches my eye and smiles.
I do not have to be a Philosopher
to know that nothing is quite what it seems.

Madam Butterfly

Huddling past the cemetery
head bent as usual to the wet pavement
I might have missed the winter cherry,

forfeited its fragile promise of
earth's unfolding
and the knowledge that it hurts to hope.

Pale blossoms pierce their prison bark,
drift on the grey sky.

I have wept for less:
a woman in a white kimono
singing to welcome death;

strewn paper petals;
a small child
treading the blood red blossoms of his grief.

If You Were Mine

If you were mine
our loving would be
rough as oyster shell
slippery as pearl.

I would close your eyes
and place on your tongue
the salt of oceans
the fruits of Persia.

If you were mine
our loving would be
playful as dolphin
plaintive as curlew.

We would join hands
on a wild shore
and teach each other
to outwit time.

Minster Lovell

They came at night, sleepwalkers,
to the sleeping ruins:
darkness moth soft, thick as nostalgia;
no moon, the willows trailing starlight,
the Windrush silent, slung between reeds,
exhaling river secrets.

They held each other close
each in their separate darkness,
feeling the blood dance wildly but
not knowing the tune;
too timid to embrace the immanence
of love or fate or future,
they turned away.

Re-visited, the ruins of their yesterday
seem quaint, obscure, archaic:
today conforms to heritage safety rules.
A sharp pragmatic sunlight
strikes the ancient stone,
trouncing their tender re-enactment.
The place belongs to other pilgrims,
hugging guide books and paper bags;
echoes to the shrieks of children
knee-deep in their pool behind
a little dam of stones,
and the mocking yaffle of a woodpecker
among the poplars.

What can they do but smile upon lost ghosts,
strangers now among the smooth grass paths
and well-groomed walls;
forgive them their unknowing,
release them to the river's flow
towards the end of time;
hold close and turn away once more.

Reversing

I have stopped before you startle
to my approach: ever submissive,
I am already reversing,
tacking erratically through towering waves
of buttercup, cow parsley, ragged robin
in the blind Devon lanes where hedge
means granite business.

You are the summer visitors,
the muck spreaders and the hairy shires;
boy farmers on your quads
the bully with the bull bar,
and the single parent
at the end of the no through road
always running late.

You are the old ones,
rubbing your headlamps, taking to the highways
heads barely poked above the wheel
like bracken unfurling.

You are the thrusting young, who,
oblivious to your own mortality,
and my warm ingratiating smile
are nudging and scraping past before
I creep into the treacherous hedge clippings.
Once I was like you: for me also
the road ahead stretched farther than the distance travelled
and nought to sixty meant
something altogether different.

But now my mind
engages reverse gear too readily:
a glance over my shoulder reveals
ghosts of lost competencies, memories
slithering like slow worms over warm tarmac
and those mistakes
I hoped were decently buried.
Once sleek and aerodynamic in its forward motion
my life diminishes, distorted in the rear view mirror
to something tiny, cumbersome.

Next time you judder to a halt in a narrow place
bumper to bumper with my diffidence,
cursing, revving rapidly backwards,
insouciant in your proprio-ceptive prime:
remember I too lived dangerously
once upon a time, and all I ask
is your patience while unchallenged
I advance a few more miles.

Dartmoor

The land lies wide open
like a woman taken time beyond time
yet holding still her secrets.

Wind from the west lets fall
the gift of metamorphosis
turf slipping from granite bone.

Her scars merely skin deep:
peat pass and leat, stone wall and beaten track
shaping the lost connections.

She wears her prescience
as surely as she wears her textured past
twofold transparency.

Through her desolation
move ghosts who were her intimates among
the brooding tors and crossways.

The Deer

She is all surprise, poised in the scrubby clearing
in perfect profile, a cut-out version of herself,
sharp against the dull brown winter earth.

She has arrived here through ancient thickets
of hazel, elder, birch, moss soft, stepping
lightly through rutted drifts of half-boned leaves.

I step closer, treading on the sharp arrows
of hedgerow cuttings, hoping we shall have time
to contemplate each other, make connection;

each in our own sluggish cloud of breath
caught in a shared point of space and time
acknowledging the gift, embracing stillness,

but before I am ready she has wheeled and gone
making for the trees, not hurrying,
her huge white horseshoe scut a parting moon

tacking the moss green skies. I touch granite
to relocate myself, the interloper here
in the cold March light waiting for the year to turn.

Styhead Tarn

Place prevails powerfully over time
within this hanging valley:
Coleridge is here, striding among his
dreams and visions
carrying in his makeshift oilskin knapsack
a portable inkwell and several quills.

Wind has bullied him up the stony trudge
from the saturated plain,
buffeted him over the col and dropped him
into a wide grey bowl of infinity.

The tarn lies pincered between two
frowning mountains, a desolate waymark,
grey light fidgeting on its grey water
rimmed with red sedge and grasses
of a treacherous Irish green.

Smoking buttresses tumble their scree
headlong to the valley bottom
dark-suited gangster clouds
hustle the crags of Great Gable and Great End,
loosing volleys of hail to pock the lake's pale skin.
Fifty sheep, flowing as one body,
point their black impassive faces
towards Borrowdale and the shelter of laborious walls
that stitch the sodden fields.

Two hundred winters and the squally gauze showers
still come weathering up from Wastwater
and the salt sea beyond;

so much water doing, like time, what it must:
marbling the mountains, dousing bracken fires,
drowning the ancient ways and
islanding huge cairns.

Coleridge is here, a dishevelled poet
toting an old broom handle,
tuning his senses to elemental powers,
his spirit to divinity in wilderness:
finding in this high place a turbulence
to match his own,
he proclaims to the echoing centuries
his terrible joy.

Loch Lomond

That day we fashioned a bracelet of lochs,
their names a highland litany
furling the tongue:
Holy Loch, Loch Ech, Loch Fyne
Loch Long, Loch Lomond.

The high road, the low road,
I know them well:
the long winding climb,
the pulse of expectancy,
mist rolling off the tops, the sun spinning,
the sudden trembling turn of time
from soon to now.

Too soon the steep descent
through sombre glens,
their stands of birch fox-fuzzy as nostalgia,
down to the dull flat lands,
leaving behind that long-anticipated now
like a homesick child,

We stood on the bare stony margins of
those bonny bonny banks
and I knew even then that
we were in separate places:
late in our season, in the wane
like the ghost of a moon up there
in the thin blue of afternoon.

I gathered rosehips for a memorial
foolish as a hen tucking another dead egg
under her warm breast;
after a month their scarlet globes
are dwindling on the windowsill,
still beaded with light but puckering
like wild strawberries that fall
suddenly from the stem.

Swimming the Horse to Mull

And when they have haltered the beast
and breathed into his nostrils,

they drag the boat through surf and row
till the rope snaps taut,
and the salt drops leap from the rope
like a school of frogs.

As the first wave uncurls,
combing his fetlock feathers,
he baulks, knowing his proper element;
knowing how easily he could win
this tug of war.

But when the sea strokes his belly
he whinnies and casts off,
tail streaming like kelp,
one eye rolling.

Released from gravity,
all four feet flail until he finds his stride
and canters slowly through
dense fields of seas.

The rowers lean back against the wind
marvelling as the great white shire
plunges among the little white horses
of the sound;

and when their keel bites the sand
the horse trots out

frisky as a yearling, up to the field
where he stands steaming quietly
dreaming of mer-mares

while on the sand
his huge hoof craters slowly fill,
fall in on themselves
and are erased.

Firth of Clyde

Banished to this safe huddle of houses
bleak by the firth
you learned solitude

and the silhouettes of battleships
slinking like grey wolves from their loch lairs
down grey sleeted water
to a wireless war that crackled
through your blindfold
childhood.

No convoys today
only a strutting tug, two ferries
and a small white ship
tussle with wind and wave
like toys on a pond.

Honour this place, you say
(seeing another time)
for the great ships in their proud
coming and going
the clamour of steel in the yards
and the heady empire
of the sea

all gone

and the sun out stalking the long glens all afternoon
gone now
the grey waters shivering.

Death in the Mountains

Stronger than juniper
the smell of death
meets us along the path

A horse lies belly-up
among the boulders
like a wrecked four-master.

She has voided something
bulbous and veined
that glistens in sunlight.

Grasshoppers and butterflies
have laid claim to her body's
swollen landscape;

flies explore her gentle face
and a yellow frog squats
in the dark stain that flows from her.

At a proper distance
her sleek companions
graze the deep bowl of pasture,

the tuneless tolling of bells
muffled by immensity.
High in the squinting sky

the great birds gather
sharpening their appetites
on pinnacles of stone.

Sauna by the Lake

Hunch-kneed on the higher bench like kiln-fired pots
we gather heat.
The darkening pine weeps resin at my back
and fresh sawn logs crackle in the stove,
sweetening the air with wood smoke.
A whisk of birch hangs in the steam
releasing sharp leaf scent.

The window frames a rectangle
of liquid light, bisected by four birches,
and their screen of leaf-fall filters molten gold
reflections from the amber shallows
of the bay.

Water grumbles and thumps the metal tank
with manic force: you toss a ladleful
onto the hot stones that spit and sizzle
as the loyly leaps upwards
to the ceiling; we flinch as it comes slamming back
to sting eyes, scald nostrils
and draw sweat from open pores.

Abandoning the hot oppressive gloom
I slip out to a luminous world
and cross the slatted jetty, skin smoking
in the cool evening air. I lower my body
into the lake, shuddering at the
cold seductive rise of water over belly and thigh
until at last my breasts burn hollows
in the floating sky and I cast myself gasping
into the sun's path.

The dying sun divides the lake,
its glittering excalibur
thrust straight at my heart. My life flows out
in widening circles black and silver:
I trail my pale diminished limbs
like curls of lemon peel, and thin growing things
pluck at my ankles from the ancient silt.

Afterwards, wound in warm towels, we watch
the light fade and the last skein of wood smoke
slowly vanishing,
and a lone black-throated diver on his dusk patrol
calls like a distant wolf
haunting the coming of the dark.

Closing

So this is how it will end:
in absence,
no sound, stillness so intense
that breathing is sacrilege.

A loon hollered last night
and in the morning
cranes flew over;
a new sky leaned down
and the lake trembled at its touch.

Nothing has changed
since men in caves
hunted the souls of deer and bison
on their blackened walls.

Earth turns,
rehearsing her seasons:
ice melts
and a soft wind coaxes
waxen flowers from frozen earth,
splits wood into leaf.

The sun lengthens its stride,
drives the reindeer
bucking and weeping black-fly;
children come running
blue mouthed from the forest.

Southwards from the tundra
the ruska leaps from fell to fell;
skies clamour,
winged with fugitives.

Ice gathers,
winter closes its pores again:
nothing has changed.

Only you have changed.
When you have gone so deep into a place
so deep into yourself
that time itself no longer counts,
such closing is not terrible.

Bornholm

Do not imagine you will ever find
all you are looking for:

this island comes close to heaven
yet even here the cold wind of elsewhere
blows off the sea;

sun hammers your head, salt seeps
into your bloodstream and the rock
you lean on gnaws into your back;

hopes that wheeled like exultant birds
now plunge, greedy and quarrelsome.

Do not believe in fixity:
you are composed of dancing molecules,
your edges all illusory.

Everything is in shift:
obedient to the moon, each tide aligns
and re-aligns the watery interface of
earth, air and ocean.

Transience shadows you:
the softest skin grows papery, mottles
like a letter long concealed;

one day it seems the whisper of dying cells
becomes a sullen roar.

Do not expect that life will tumble you
to a smooth finish:
almost but not quite is the rule,

death the only model of perfection.

Pyhaniemi: Noon

The boat rests on floating cloud
its worn red blades dipping and rising
dripping small fishbite rings on a glassy sky.

There is a faint undulation
akin to the slow breathing of the earth,
the lake tremulous like parachute silk.

A tern haunting the shallows screams
disapproval, flicking its forked tail.
A drowning dragonfly flails its way to shore.

Small puffs of white cloud have assembled
in lines and marched southwards like boys
innocent of death destined for war.

All morning they have come and come
joining and growing sullen and grey-bellied
conjuring fretful winds that pucker the lake

like honeycomb, banish the fledgling birds,
weave a rough herring bone tweed of water,
rattle the alders and slap waves on the shore.

And the winds die suddenly and the ducks
resume their skittish circumnavigation
but nothing is the same for summer has passed.

Sunday Morning in Orta

In the square a melancholy
yellowing of leaves;
muffling of footfall
among waiting tables;
rapid fire of boatmen
hustling for custom;
boats rocking out of time
as the wake catches them.

Outside the café Venus
language drifts and slaps
like sleepy lake wash
over the warm slipway;
the mountain air is soft
a child on the jetty cries
'look at me! look at me!'

Across the lake in Pella
the hour strikes early;
soon from hill to hill
the bells are jostling time,
their syncopated tolling
dissonant by half a tone.

San Nicolao San Filiberto
San Maurizio d'Opaglio
each campanile claims
allegiance to its own
frescoed assembly of
androgynous saints
embracing painted agonies.

Outside the café Venus
the last echo drowns
in Sunday somnolence
and life like time itself
seems an inexact science
best celebrated with
a glass of dark Barolo
and a face upturned
to the forgiving sun.

The Nunnery: Iona

In the soft blessing of full-moon
the ghosts of well-born canonesses
pass modestly among
imagined cloisters

treading a silver herb-strewn path
between the rounded archways
of refectory and church.

They are time's shadows
half apprehended in
the liminal transparency of night

unmindful of those savage winds
from the north
that unleashed storms to swallow the moon
and moaned among
the cracks of their souls

and the ceaseless flagellation of rain
on backs bent for the love of God
to patient endeavour

unmindful too of those warm winds
from the west
and how they welcomed
the smallest uninvited flowers
their sisters in survival
clinging to the stern stones

and how they tucked up their skirts
and ran barefoot over the coarse turf
to a silver shore
and gathered shells with little birdlike
cries of delight.

The Last Monk

When the last candle gutters and fails

when there is no music but the plainsong
of the wind in the rafters

when the faithful stones
soft and grey like pigeon plumage
lie open to the plundering sky

when my swollen knees are the last
to shape the prayer-worn hollows
at the altar

when there is none left to remember
novice feet hop-scotching down
the street of the dead
for joy of a harvest moon

I, the last soul on the island,
shall set sail

having fashioned a boat
curved and caulked for the final journey

looking for landfall beyond the veil

beyond saints
beyond certainties
solid as green marble

blue as eternity

Enough

I strode over crisp turf
beached with blown sand

towards wild headlands that
shouldered an ocean to the west

weaving a sinuous way among
crags and spongy hollows

keeping north
the sea always to my left

a jealous raven claimed his airspace
over that blind hinterland

I lay on a scratchy bed of last year's heather
beside a small rock lively with light

and watched white surf flowering
at the edge of time

sipped salt on the wind

I left the first primrose in its damp hermit's cell
knowing that I had come at last

to a place that was enough

16 Train
20 Out of your mind
45